SHAPE
ME A RHYME

Nature's Forms in Poetry

Jane Yolen

Photographs by

Jason Stemple

WORDSONG

Wordsong
An Imprint of Boyds Mills Press, Inc.
815 Church Street
Honesdale, Pennsylvania 18431
Printed in China

Library of Congress Cataloging-in-Publication Data

Yolen, Jane.
  Shape me a rhyme : nature's forms in poetry / poems by Jane Yolen ;
photographs by Jason Stemple.
      p. cm.
  ISBN 978-1-59078-450-1 (alk. paper)
 1. Geometry in nature—Juvenile poetry. 2. Nature—Juvenile poetry.
3. Shapes—Juvenile poetry. 4. Children's poetry, American. I. Stemple,
Jason, ill. II. Title.
  PS3575.O43S53 2007
  811'.54—dc22
                                    2006101463

First edition
The text of this book is set in 20-point Palatino.

10 9 8 7 6 5 4 3 2 1

For Caroline and Amelia,
who know all these shapes
— J.Y.

For my dad, who's always with me
— J.S.

Contents

A Note from the Author

After my son Jason Stemple and I produced *Color Me a Rhyme* and *Count Me a Rhyme*—two books of concept poems with photographs—the question arose: what should we do next?

A book of poems about shapes seemed a perfect companion to those two. However, shapes in nature are never exactly perfect, and so we knew we might have a tough time finding all the shapes we wished for.

A circle was simple—the sun. It was the first photo and poem we agreed upon. The crescent moon was another natural. We discovered heart-shaped leaves from a tree on Jason's front lawn but even better ones in a forested area close to his home. An alligator showing its triangular teeth was fairly easy to find since Jason lives in South Carolina, where alligators also reside.

Other shapes in the natural world proved to be much harder to come upon, such as the square and coil. So we used our imaginations.

As with the first two books, the photographs usually came before the poems. But the poems had to take on a life of their own. Often I threw away my first and second and third efforts, trying to match the beauty of Jason's photographs. I wanted to do more than just talk about the shape. I wanted to also set down how the shape made me feel.

By looking at Jason's beautiful pictures, you, too, can come up with your own poems. Plus, around each poem I've included extra words that describe that particular shape.

—*Jane Yolen*

Circle

Round as a ball,
Round as the sun,
A circle goes round
To where it's begun.

Where it's begun
Is where it will end,
And then it starts circling
Over again.

round

halo

circuit

sphere

orbit

loop

9

Triangle

To tell the truth,
The gator's tooth—
Triangular in shape—
Is dangerous
And dagger-ous
When that great mouth's agape.

triform

pyramid

deltoid

whorl

spiral

curl

Coil

Tight as
a spring,
ready, set,
load—
the coil is just
waiting
till it can
EXPLODE.

curlicue

twist

Star

Five points,
the super star-
fish shines
in the sea.
Are those all
arms
or are those
legs
clinging
on to me?

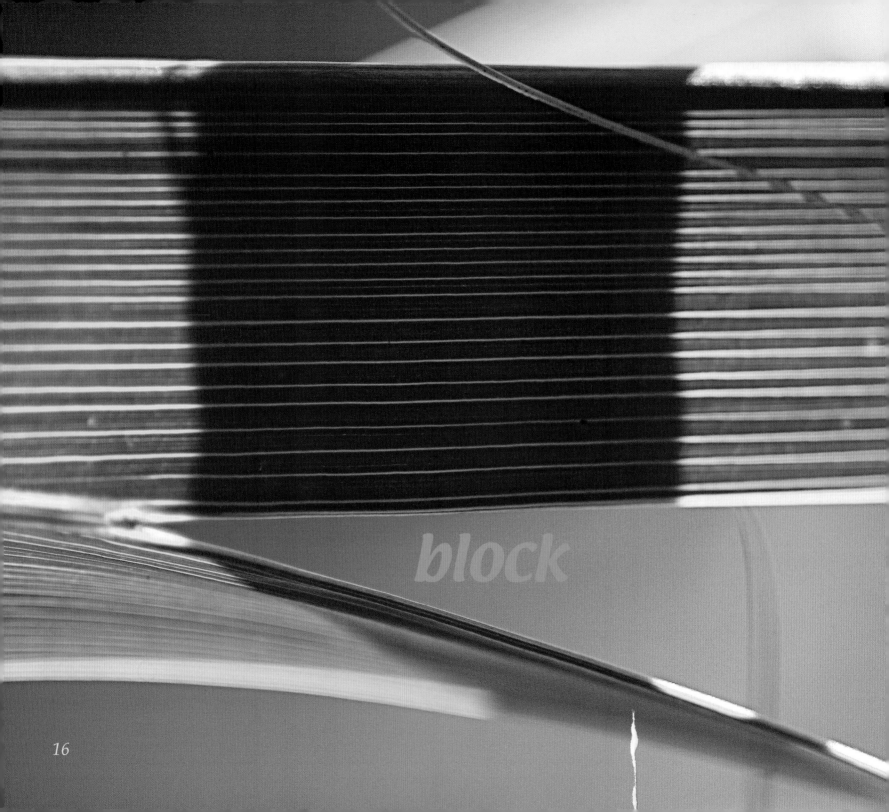

Square

A shadow square
Upon a frond
Resides beside
A quiet pond.

Since nature rarely
Seeds a square,
We must make do
With what is there.

tetragon

quadrangle

quadrate

quad

Heart

Hearts are not always red,
Not always full of love,
Not always beating steadily.
Some hearts fall from above.
Dry, solo, autumn-hued,
The still heart of a tree
Settles on the leafy ground
For all eternity.

valentine

19

Arch: A Haiku

Arch a sand dollar
Well above the high-tide line,
You will get back change.

span

curve

bend

bow

21

Wave

Lazy curl,
Wind-blown hair,
In the palm fronds
Everywhere.

Who can comb
The wavy tangle?
Let it go
And watch it dangle.

eddy

billow

roller

surge

Oval

ovoid

An oval
fits eggs-actly
inside
an airy nest
so it can nestle
tight against
its mother's
feathered breast.

25

outspread

splay

Fan

A single shell,
A jingle shell,
Just like an open hand.
A single shell,
A dingle shell,
Fanned out upon the sand.

quadrilateral

Rectangle

How does a spider,
Weaving a strand,
Make a rectangle?
Is it all planned?

Or does that small spider,
Hand over head,
Make a rectangle
Untangling its web?

orthogonal

oblong

Crescent

Oh moon, you are not new
Or full and round,
Just a sliver of light
Shining down.
Your shape, like the side
Of a copper cent,
Out of pocket but
Not yet spent.

sickle

semicircle

lunate

About the
Author
and
Photographer

Jane Yolen has written almost three hundred books, many of them award winners. Four months a year she lives in St. Andrews, Scotland, seeking out castles, Pictish stones, and bagpipes. She spends the rest of her time traveling, visiting her grandchildren in South Carolina and Minnesota, and at her home in Hatfield, Massachusetts.

Jason Stemple is a free-lance photographer whose work has appeared in a number of books for young readers, including the acclaimed *Color Me a Rhyme* and *Count Me a Rhyme*, poetry books by his mother, Jane Yolen. He lives with his wife, Joanne, and their twin daughters in Charleston, South Carolina.